VIOLA

101 MOST BEAUTIFUL SONGS

Available for
FLUTE, CLARINET, ALTO SAX, TENOR SAX, TRUMPET,
HORN, TROMBONE, VIOLIN, VIOLA, CELLO

ISBN 978-1-5400-4827-1

Visit Hal Leonard Online at
www.halleonard.com

World headquarters, contact:
Hal Leonard
7777 West Bluemound Road
Milwaukee, WI 53213
Email: info@halleonard.com

In Europe, contact:
Hal Leonard Europe Limited
1 Red Place
London, W1K 6PL
Email: info@halleonardeurope.com

In Australia, contact:
Hal Leonard Australia Pty. Ltd.
4 Lentara Court
Cheltenham, Victoria, 3192 Australia
Email: info@halleonard.com.au

CONTENTS

ALWAYS

VIOLA

Words and Music by
IRVING BERLIN

ALWAYS ON MY MIND

VIOLA

Words and Music by WAYNE THOMPSON,
MARK JAMES and JOHNNY CHRISTOPHER

AND I LOVE HER

VIOLA

Words and Music by JOHN LENNON
and PAUL McCARTNEY

AND I LOVE YOU SO

VIOLA

Words and Music by
DON McLEAN

Moderately

AND SO IT GOES

VIOLA

Words and Music by
BILLY JOEL

Slow Ballad, with much rubato

ANNIE'S SONG

VIOLA

Words and Music by
JOHN DENVER

ANYWHERE IS

VIOLA

Words and Music by ENYA,
NICKY RYAN and ROMA RYAN

BEIN' GREEN

VIOLA

Words and Music by
JOE RAPOSO

Slowly, reflectively

BLACKBIRD

VIOLA

Words and Music by JOHN LENNON
and PAUL McCARTNEY

Slowly and smoothly

THE BOOK OF LOVE

VIOLA

Words and Music by
STEPHIN MERRITT

CODA

THE BOXER

VIOLA

Words and Music by
PAUL SIMON

BRING HIM HOME
from LES MISÉRABLES

VIOLA

Music by CLAUDE-MICHEL SCHÖNBERG
Lyrics by HERBERT KRETZMER and ALAIN BOUBLIL

BY THE TIME I GET TO PHOENIX

VIOLA

Words and Music by
JIMMY WEBB

CANDLE IN THE WIND

VIOLA

Words and Music by ELTON JOHN
and BERNIE TAUPIN

A CHILD IS BORN

VIOLA

By THAD JONES

(They Long to Be)
CLOSE TO YOU

VIOLA

Lyrics by HAL DAVID
Music by BURT BACHARACH

CITY OF STARS

from LA LA LAND

VIOLA

Music by JUSTIN HURWITZ
Lyrics by BENJ PASEK & JUSTIN PAUL

Slower

rit.

COME SUNDAY
from BLACK, BROWN & BEIGE

By DUKE ELLINGTON

VIOLA

CRAZY

VIOLA

Words and Music by
WILLIE NELSON

CRYING

VIOLA

Words and Music by ROY ORBISON
and JOE MELSON

Moderately slow, with feeling

DREAM A LITTLE DREAM OF ME

VIOLA

Words by GUS KAHN
Music by WILBUR SCHWANDT
and FABIAN ANDREE

DAUGHTERS

VIOLA

Words and Music by
JOHN MAYER

D.S. al Coda

CODA

EASY LIVING
Theme from the Paramount Picture EASY LIVING

VIOLA

Words and Music by LEO ROBIN
and RALPH RAINGER

ETERNAL FLAME

VIOLA

Words and Music by BILLY STEINBERG,
TOM KELLY and SUSANNA HOFFS

ETERNALLY

VIOLA

Words by GEOFFREY PARSONS
Music by CHARLES CHAPLIN

Slowly, with feeling

EVERY BREATH YOU TAKE

VIOLA

Music and Lyrics by
STING

(EVERYTHING I DO) I DO IT FOR YOU

from the Motion Picture ROBIN HOOD: PRINCE OF THIEVES

VIOLA

Written by MICHAEL KAMEN

Moderately slow

FEELING GOOD

from THE ROAR OF THE GREASEPAINT – THE SMELL OF THE CROWD

VIOLA

Words and Music by LESLIE BRICUSSE
and ANTHONY NEWLEY

FOR ALL WE KNOW

VIOLA

Words by SAM M. LEWIS
Music by J. FRED COOTS

Slowly

GABRIEL'S OBOE

from the Motion Picture THE MISSION

VIOLA

Words and Music by
ENNIO MORRICONE

Slowly, expressively

GOOD NIGHT

VIOLA

Words and Music by JOHN LENNON
and PAUL McCARTNEY

GOODNIGHT, SWEETHEART, GOODNIGHT
(Goodnight, It's Time to Go)

VIOLA

Words and Music by JAMES HUDSON
and CALVIN CARTER

HAVE I TOLD YOU LATELY

VIOLA

Words and Music by
VAN MORRISON

HELLO

VIOLA

Words and Music by
LIONEL RICHIE

Slow Ballad

HEAL THE WORLD

VIOLA

Words and Music by
MICHAEL JACKSON

D.S. al Coda

CODA

HERE, THERE AND EVERYWHERE

VIOLA

Words and Music by JOHN LENNON
and PAUL McCARTNEY

Moderately slow

HIGHLAND CATHEDRAL

VIOLA

By MICHAEL KORB
and ULRICH ROEVER

Stately March, in 2

I HAVE A DREAM

from MAMMA MIA!

VIOLA

Words and Music by BENNY ANDERSSON
and BJÖRN ULVAEUS

D.S. al Coda

CODA

I LEFT MY HEART IN SAN FRANCISCO

VIOLA

Words by DOUGLASS CROSS
Music by GEORGE CORY

I WILL

VIOLA

Words and Music by JOHN LENNON
and PAUL McCARTNEY

I'LL BE AROUND

VIOLA

Words and Music by
ALEC WILDER

Slowly, with expression

I'LL BE SEEING YOU

from RIGHT THIS WAY

VIOLA

Written by IRVING KAHAL
and SAMMY FAIN

Moderately slow

I'VE DREAMED OF YOU

VIOLA

Words and Music by ANN HAMPTON CALLAWAY
and ROLF LOVLAND

IN MY ROOM

VIOLA

Words and Music by BRIAN WILSON
and GARY USHER

LA VIE EN ROSE
(Take Me to Your Heart Again)

VIOLA

Original French Lyrics by EDITH PIAF
Music by LUIGUY
English Lyrics by MACK DAVID

Slowly, with expression

JUST GIVE ME A REASON

VIOLA

Words and Music by ALECIA MOORE,
JEFF BHASKER and NATE RUESS

CODA

LADY IN RED

VIOLA

Words and Music by
CHRIS DeBURGH

Moderately slow

Play 3 times

LET IT BE ME
(Je t'appartiens)

VIOLA

English Words by MANN CURTIS
French Words by PIERRE DeLANOE
Music by GILBERT BECAUD

Moderately

LOST IN YOUR EYES

VIOLA

Words and Music by
DEBORAH GIBSON

LOVE ME TENDER

VIOLA

Words and Music by ELVIS PRESLEY
and VERA MATSON

Moderately slow

LOVING YOU

VIOLA

Words and Music by JERRY LEIBER
and MIKE STOLLER

Slowly, with a beat

LULLABYE
(Goodnight, My Angel)

VIOLA

Words and Music by
BILLY JOEL

Rubato, gently

MIA & SEBASTIAN'S THEME

from LA LA LAND

VIOLA

Music by
JUSTIN HURWITZ

MICHELLE

VIOLA

Words and Music by JOHN LENNON
and PAUL McCARTNEY

MONA LISA

from the Paramount Picture CAPTAIN CAREY, U.S.A.

VIOLA

Words and Music by JAY LIVINGSTON
and RAY EVANS

MY FOOLISH HEART

VIOLA

Words by NED WASHINGTON
Music by VICTOR YOUNG

Slowly and expressively

MY FUNNY VALENTINE
from BABES IN ARMS

VIOLA

Words by LORENZ HART
Music by RICHARD RODGERS

MY VALENTINE

VIOLA

Words and Music by
PAUL McCARTNEY

MY WAY

VIOLA

English Words by PAUL ANKA
Original French Words by GILLES THIBAULT
Music by JACQUES REVAUX and CLAUDE FRANCOIS

NANCY WITH THE LAUGHING FACE

VIOLA

Words by PHIL SILVERS
Music by JAMES VAN HEUSEN

NATURE BOY

VIOLA

Words and Music by
EDEN AHBEZ

NEVER ENOUGH

from THE GREATEST SHOWMAN

VIOLA

Words and Music by BENJ PASEK
and JUSTIN PAUL

A NIGHTINGALE SANG IN BERKELEY SQUARE

VIOLA

Lyric by ERIC MASCHWITZ
Music by MANNING SHERWIN

PERFECT

VIOLA

Words and Music by
ED SHEERAN

PHOTOGRAPH

VIOLA

Words and Music by ED SHEERAN,
JOHNNY McDAID, MARTIN PETER HARRINGTON
and TOM LEONARD

Moderately

THE PLACE WHERE LOST THINGS GO

from MARY POPPINS RETURNS

VIOLA

Music by MARC SHAIMAN
Lyrics by SCOTT WITTMAN and MARC SHAIMAN

RAINY DAYS AND MONDAYS

VIOLA

Lyrics by PAUL WILLIAMS
Music by ROGER NICHOLS

RELEASE ME

VIOLA

Words and Music by ROBERT YOUNT,
EDDIE MILLER and DUB WILLIAMS

Moderately slow

REWRITE THE STARS
from THE GREATEST SHOWMAN

VIOLA

Words and Music by BENJ PASEK
and JUSTIN PAUL

SAILING

VIOLA

Words and Music by
CHRISTOPHER CROSS

SCARBOROUGH FAIR/CANTICLE

VIOLA

Arrangement and Original Counter Melody by
PAUL SIMON and ARTHUR GARFUNKEL

SHALLOW

from A STAR IS BORN

VIOLA

Words and Music by STEFANI GERMANOTTA,
MARK RONSON, ANDREW WYATT
and ANTHONY ROSSOMANDO

Moderately

SINCE I DON'T HAVE YOU

VIOLA

Words and Music by JAMES BEAUMONT,
JANET VOGEL, JOSEPH VERSCHAREN,
WALTER LESTER, LENNIE MARTIN,
JOSEPH ROCK and JOHN TAYLOR

Slowly, with a strong, rockin' beat

SHE'S ALWAYS A WOMAN

VIOLA

Words and Music by
BILLY JOEL

Quickly, in 1

SMILE
Theme from MODERN TIMES

VIOLA

Words by JOHN TURNER and GEOFFREY PARSONS
Music by CHARLES CHAPLIN

Moderately, with great warmth

SMOKE GETS IN YOUR EYES

from ROBERTA

VIOLA

Words by OTTO HARBACH
Music by JEROME KERN

SOMETHING WONDERFUL

from THE KING AND I

VIOLA

Lyrics by OSCAR HAMMERSTEIN II
Music by RICHARD RODGERS

SOMEWHERE

from WEST SIDE STORY

VIOLA

Lyrics by STEPHEN SONDHEIM
Music by LEONARD BERNSTEIN

THE SOUND OF SILENCE

VIOLA

Words and Music by
PAUL SIMON

STARDUST

VIOLA

Words by MITCHELL PARISH
Music by HOAGY CARMICHAEL

STRANGERS IN THE NIGHT

adapted from A MAN COULD GET KILLED

VIOLA

Words by CHARLES SINGLETON
and EDDIE SNYDER
Music by BERT KAEMPFERT

SWAY
(Quien será)

VIOLA

English Words by NORMAN GIMBEL
Spanish Words and Music by PABLO BELTRÁN RUIZ
and LUIS DEMETRIO TRACONIS MOLINA

TENNESSEE WALTZ

VIOLA

Words and Music by REDD STEWART
and PEE WEE KING

(THERE IS) NO GREATER LOVE

VIOLA

Words by MARTY SYMES
Music by ISHAM JONES

With emotion

THEY SAY IT'S WONDERFUL

from the Stage Production ANNIE GET YOUR GUN

VIOLA

Words and Music by
IRVING BERLIN

THREE TIMES A LADY

VIOLA

Words and Music by
LIONEL RICHIE

TIME TO SAY GOODBYE

VIOLA

Words by LUCIO QUARANTOTTO
and FRANK PETERSON
Music by FRANCESCO SARTORI

Slowly

(small notes optional)

TRUE COLORS

VIOLA

Words and Music by BILLY STEINBERG
and TOM KELLY

TRULY

VIOLA

Words and Music by
LIONEL RICHIE

UNEXPECTED SONG

from SONG & DANCE

VIOLA

Music by ANDREW LLOYD WEBBER
Lyrics by DON BLACK

WE'VE ONLY JUST BEGUN

VIOLA

Words and Music by ROGER NICHOLS
and PAUL WILLIAMS

WE'VE GOT TONIGHT

VIOLA

Words and Music by
BOB SEGER

WHAT A WONDERFUL WORLD

VIOLA

Words and Music by GEORGE DAVID WEISS
and BOB THIELE

WONDERFUL TONIGHT

VIOLA

Words and Music by
ERIC CLAPTON

YESTER-ME, YESTER-YOU, YESTERDAY

VIOLA

Words by RON MILLER
Music by BRYAN WELLS

YESTERDAY ONCE MORE

VIOLA

Words and Music by JOHN BETTIS
and RICHARD CARPENTER

YESTERDAY, WHEN I WAS YOUNG
(Hier Encore)

VIOLA

English Lyric by HERBERT KRETZMER
Original French Text and Music by CHARLES AZNAVOUR

YOU ARE THE SUNSHINE OF MY LIFE

VIOLA

Words and Music by
STEVIE WONDER

YOU'RE THE INSPIRATION

VIOLA

Words and Music by PETER CETERA
and DAVID FOSTER

YOUNG AT HEART

from YOUNG AT HEART

VIOLA

Words by CAROLYN LEIGH
Music by JOHNNY RICHARDS

YOUR SONG

VIOLA

Words and Music by ELTON JOHN
and BERNIE TAUPIN